FOR YOUR OWN GOOD

Caitlin Press Inc.
8100 Alderwood Road,
Halfmoon Bay, BC V0N 1Y1
www.caitlin-press.com

Text design by Benjamin Dunfield
Cover concept and design by Andrea Routley and Vici Johnstone
Edited by Rachel Rose
Cover art by Thomas Shahan
Printed in Canada

Caitlin Press Inc. acknowledges financial support from the Government of Canada through the Canada Book Fund and the Canada Council for the Arts, and from the Province of British Columbia through the British Columbia Arts Council and the Book Publisher's Tax Credit.

Canada Council   Conseil des Arts   BRITISH COLUMBIA
for the Arts   du Canada   ARTS COUNCIL

Library and Archives Canada Cataloguing in Publication

Horlick, Leah, author
    For your own good / Leah Horlick.

Poems.
ISBN 978-1-927575-67-3 (pbk.)
    I. Title.

PS8615.O745F67 2015   C811'.6   C2015-900168-4

FOR YOUR OWN GOOD

Leah Horlick

CAITLIN PRESS

For Calondra, who believed.

TABLE OF CONTENTS

VANISHING ACT

I say
Do what you are going to do, and I will tell about it.
—*Sharon Olds, "I Go Back To May 1937"*

THE CIRCUS

All those nights camped out in the field, squinting
for a light, a flicker, calliope in the grass.
Grease and fire, they'd understand
and tuck you into their silken fold. They'd fawn
and dress you, glitter and eventually parade.
You bought your ticket, held your flag at the front
of the empty line, shut your eyes.
If you counted to one hundred, they'd appear.
Every ninety-nine you opened up to silence.
The field was set on fire and still you stood, wedded
to your acrobats, the promise of trapeze and escape
artists, soon. Your body changed and bled and the year came
when you knew you would die on the highway,
in a truck bed, in a grain silo, tied to a fence, in a slough,
at your own hand. You left to find them.

RINGMASTER

There's an alleyway, and a secret place,
    and you know it's right because the books

tell you as an invert, all your love stories begin
    in hiding. And you love her because she is angles

and shoulders, twin blue yard lights for eyes. How her teeth gleam
    sharp when she throws those hoops in the air, how the listeners

leap to twist through them, flames so close they singe
    your hair. She wears a horse's bridle on her

left wrist to signal she is not to be kept, and she blisters
    under its chafe. One night you reel her

into a corner with a bandage. She says she thought you
    were going to kiss her, she doesn't love women

but anything could happen. She has a talent, dreams
    the future, won't reveal the one

that wakes her with you in it. But it's closing night. She has an empty
    seat, passenger side, with your name on it. You say *of course,*

because you have a backpack, a matching ring of red
    skin around your wrist, and you thought you'd never find her.

Vanishing Act

She can't let anyone know
    you worship her, so for your first act

you intend to learn to let her touch you in secret—
    on the highway, in a truck bed, a grain silo,

against the fence, beside the slough, beneath
    your own small hand. All the places

you were meant to die as a girl, and she says she'll
    protect you. You sleep in the truck, her one arm

around you so tight, bottle of Hot 100 tucked
    in her child-sized fist, while the farms grow

crystal meth and wheat around you, silent.

GROOMING

Spook. That's what she calls it—
how you shrink from her hands.

Like a horse. Spook. As if you only
need steadiness, lumps of sugar.

For her to pull on your mouth
to tell you where to go.

Fortune Teller

A morning for apologies. Bedside,
    she names you talisman, charm
against her nightmares. Casts herself,

magnesium and heat, as your *catalyst*.
    You're special. She could tell
just by looking.

And you should feel special, here
    with the mirror's flat nest
of glass, your breast speckled red

with quarter-sized abrasions, blue nickels
    across your waist. The square edge
of her beltbuckle, a shadow—her fingers

too slow and rye-swollen to undress
    herself, or you. She was sure
you would like it. She could tell

just by looking. All the omens gathered
    to foretell your future—blood
vessels feathering,

sparrows beneath your collarbone, hair
    of the dog, the mirror flat and bright
and clear.

FEVER SPELL

Food poisoning, or alcohol, again,
or guilt—too soon to tell.

You are still among the firsts, trying
yes, and women, and each other.

Poison or shame has doubled her
over the tiles, dry-heaving

behind the wall where you unfold
from the night with a different nausea.

Your jeans in the corner, hollow
as if you ascended, or were pressed

out of yourself from her weight.
It is your fault, or alcohol's,

your newness, your body's refusal
of her. You made her do it, this

the unnatural act, and you're what
has to break before her fever.

GHOST HOUSE

Because you are broken, she moves you
    into the house of cracked things—

faucets, aquariums, lamps on
    the nightstand, then off again.

Because you will never be enough, she moves
    you into the house of what she can measure—

water heaters, electrical meters, thermostat
    and ticking dial.

And because you are of a kind, the house knows
    you. When you cry out,

the lights flicker, ghostly blue and ragged.
    When she says you are *shut off,*

the light switches nod their white tiny
    heads. Tiles creak *yes* beneath her

edicts—*something bad must have happened
    to make you this way,* the way

where you don't want her. But the windows
    rattle, disagree. In their honeyed,

blindless light, they see it—something bad
    is *happening.*

CAPTIVITY

She names herself keeper, alpha. Grabs
    your breasts to make you hiss for strangers.

You're the mirror that makes her look skinny, the whip
    she cracks for show. Nightly, she wants fireworks,

and you learn to fake them out of whiskey and sharp red nails
    until the neighbouring creatures shake their cages

in fear, or applaud. She turns your body into an animal
    you don't understand. When you're good,

she says, you purr. She could mean tabby, or engine.
    When you're mewling or worse, when you're *no*,

it's the silent treatment until you climb the walls
    for her touch, until any word is a scrap, even

when she comes home with that other smell on her, even
    when she says she loves you, until you believe it.

THE DISAPPEARING WOMAN

With her new magic, she makes you
	invisible.

The women with black eyes
	do not see you, in your bare

sleeves, your tired, unmarked face.
	The women with black eyes

can say *doorknob*. Can say *staircase*
	and *fell down*.

She doesn't give you black eyes, and
	the doctors do not see her, not in your

long hair, your good earrings, in your quiet
	descriptions of pain. They would say

boyfriend. They would see *husband*. She
	does not give you black eyes,

she is not your husband, and you do not
	say anything.

LITTLE VOICE

That morning in the motel
    where your best friend lived,
new snow outside, at least in the memory

and the stranger—he was eighteen,
    you were alone, she was downstairs
at the pop machine or something

while you watched the snow, the nest
    of beached antlers in the yard
behind the pine trees and then he was there, too

in the room, telling you about
    a guitar, or something useless
and you thought

empty room, you thought *quiet house,*
    you were a very smart girl and you felt
the footstep he took one step closer behind you

at the window, and from the rising star
    of your gut you heard it, like twin
drops of water—you have to leave the room

Right. Now. And quietly, and you did.
    That was *smart.* You were a *smart*
girl, and you did not tell anyone

not when they found out he was
in her room at night, not
when they sent him away, not

until you were a grown woman, and what
you wouldn't give
for that little voice again, now.

STARFISH

It will take you years to know this body
grown in brushfire, backyard acres.

Your skin dark but never enough. Eyes the old deer-plus-highbeams.
Your mouth is for lipstick and thumb for hitchhiking, never
at the same time.

Breasts are *the parts that get cancer.* Sex is not the same as what
happened to your neighbour in the car outside of town.

Your mostly-whiteness protects you, but not from the boys
who whisper behind you at the movies, snap your bra straps. The girl who
throws you against the bathroom wall, calls you a dyke.

You are afraid of everyone. Your nickname is *hermit crab.*
Come out of your shell, they say.

You never know which part they mean. Everywhere feels so soft.

You name yourself a starfish: radiating, symmetrical. All of you stems
from the hidden salt of your mouth.

You are covered in small bear-trap structures and made only of arms.
You can shed all your limbs to escape a predator.

You can regenerate anything
given time.

SUIT OF FEATHERS

[It]does me no good to be good to me now;
violence has changed me.
—Louise Glück, "October"

THE SUN

When she's away, you have the house, your days
    to split open like peaches—

full and bright, solid at the centre. You don't
    have to share. Grow your hair a little

longer and leave the windows open, the door
    swung out on its hinges. Make cold amber

tea, plant heart's-ease at the crest
    of the sidewalk. In the evenings, you let

the cat out on a tether, sit with the old quilt
    across your brown knees, watch someone

in the next driveway fiddle with a car, wave
    at the traffic. Or you ride your bike, remember

your legs. Find the one hill in town and canter
    to its nape, lie slant in the grass until sweat

pools at your clavicle. You draw the Sun card over
    and over, and again on your body.

Ride back on the last edge of light
    and a breeze. The cat waits for you

in the window. The neighbour's engine runs
    at last. You clear the front steps in one

stride and a rare smile. *Holy shit,* he tells you.
You look so happy. Yes, you say,

I know. And she can hear the glow of you
through the phone, asks *It's because*

I'm gone, isn't it?

For Your Own Good

The cats are a test. First,
you have to catch them—brown
and grey flashes in the barn, soft-pawed,
pouncing across sawdust.

Left alone with her mother,
you bring two handfuls of kitten to the raw
table. They squirm and curl against
your sweater. You can't yet grab creatures
by the back of the neck the way
she taught you—

It's fine! You won't hurt them! This
is how their mothers do it.
You still flinch, afraid of being
scratched, or worse and what else
lives in this barn—owls, mice,

even her mother. When the horses
come in at night, how you press
yourself flat to the edge of the stall.

We're going to vaccinate the kittens
down at the barn. You've practised saying it
all day, worked yourself up. If you try
you can almost drawl.

Her mother brings out the long needle,
speaks to you in a voice so quiet you know
it's for the cats. Your job is to hold them.

Her mother's hands are red
and steady. She finds a loose nook of fur,
presses the syringe down, kittens
purring the whole time. *See? Easy.*

Years from now, you think of her,
cat who walks by herself. Once, she must
have been a flash in that barn, learning
what was cruel, what was for your own
good.

SUIT OF FEATHERS

1. PEREGRINE

You are trying to decide if you will go with her, for good, this time
    through the morning-dark grid of semis and orange lights,

oil fires and freight yards. Like most, you came here first
    to drink on the cusp of eighteen. Dressed in black,

fed gin and grenadine at the goth bar, you listened to industrial, the signs
    that told you not to snort coke in the bathroom. No one listens

to those signs in Alberta, now. With all that rolled-up money the city courts
    her. You drive the long stretch and count the rigs

drilling their beaks into the fields, come up with reasons,
    and throw them back to the ground again.

2. Chickenhawk

In the single room you rent because it's cheaper,
    where no one will know you're a couple, where

you sneak her bags up the back stairs, she tells you
    we could live here. It's legal in Alberta—

stripping. She knows you've thought about it.
    Some women, *you can tell just by watching them.*

You can pay off my student loan.
    When you ask her if she knows

what the definition of a pimp is,
    like in that one Michelle Tea poem,

where all her friends want her to trick
    so they can go for smoothies again,

she rolls into the wall, won't talk.
    She hasn't read that poem.

There's no word for this woman. Not madam, cougar
    or chickenhawk. You can tell just by watching her.

3. RAVEN

In the morgue for birds at the university
    of Alberta, the smell of freezer burn

and blood, feathers, and the way she touches them
    turns you. Sceptre of a frozen eagle.

Silver cabinet full of falcons. You don't ask
    to see the raven, only imagine the shelter

of its frostbitten wingspan. You stand in the hall,
    elbows tight against your ribs,

watch coils of steam circle her feet,
    the hands and talons.

The birds are safe here, flightless,
    sharp and cold, kept from rotting.

Nothing is wasted. If you move here, for her, she tells you
    to write your will, common law.

She asks what you would leave to her. You look
    at the birds, and think, *nothing*.

4. BUZZARD

You knew it was bad. But not like this.
    Late afternoon walk down Whyte and already they're at you.

The man as big as you both side-by-each and day drunk
    blocks your path—*Can I ask you a question?*

No, you tell him, push past. You can feel the fear
    molting from her like feathers. It's your fault.

You're the confirmation, your long hair, those shoes
    beside her. Outside the good restaurant

with the sidewalk line up, outdoor patio, west-facing
    windows to catch the oil money, the sunset

a man sticks his tongue between
    two fingers and calls you for what you are.

Yes. You wheel and turn, *make a scene.* You are not
    scared anymore, until you look ahead

and see her shouldering away from you,
    head down, through the crowd.

5. Sparrow

You find her at the entrance to that antique shop
    you both liked. Where you buy the white mugs

with the koi fish, blue scales feathered into china.
    This is not the first time she will tell you

to be quiet. *You made us look*
    just as bad as he did.

6. Vulture

In the cards you hide from her under the bed,
    you keep drawing seven feathers:

two birds at feast on another, nearby
    train tracks, the bones not yet clean.

And then that other vulture, circling
    in the corner—wheeling over trains

while you are picked apart
    by your own kind. Vulture, you

will tell this story again and again
    to feed yourself. If only you had done

something. You could see it
    all along. Well, feast in your own

way, vulture. Someone needs to be
    the witness, unable to look away
from the wreck.

THE YELLOW SCARF

makes you look like a brown person, she tells you,
since when have you been brown? And in the dress you're straight
and the hat makes you look like an immigrant but your breasts are
coined with raisins, your skin is the colour of cinnamon. You are food.
Your children will be Vikings, she's talking to her brother about the
turkey baster already but you are seven generations of women who hid
under the kitchen table from horses and men and how is this any
different? You and your grandmothers will be gone before anyone
notices, faster than you can say
Jew.

SEVEN OF SWORDS
Blue Lounge, Cologne

You have to walk past *Hombres* and *Boners* and the *Mr. Leather Bear*
parade complete with sash to get to the only dyke bar
in Cologne. Cathedral towers lean over the whole city, peer
down those basement steps. You are all embarrassed
at the red leather, how you can still smoke inside, how
there is nowhere to hide here, from women. Every time
someone looks sideways you blush like a broken vessel. You could
do whatever you want. You are so far away. She would
never have to know. The tallest butch in the room
nods at you. She is wearing sunglasses *inside*.
At night. She and her cigarette are not deterred
by your long hair. You are not drunk enough
to forget your send-off of tears and *Do whatever*
you want in Europe, ok, whatever the Fuck You
want. You don't.

THE TOWER
Lobkowicz Palace, Prague Castle

From the tower, Prague severs into little squares—orange
for roof, grey for sky, empty spaces for your fingers to wind
through. Windows wired off in case pigeons squat or people
jump. Below you the muddy river and more square stones,
the cemetery and its twelve heavy layers. Dead everywhere
and low clouds of rain. To get here, you climbed for hours
across Europe, dropped coins into hungry cathedral boxes,
stood with silent hands while other women crossed their hearts.
In the hostel dark they talk about first love and you sink into
yourself like a crowded grave. There's no room for your body here.
When you cry in Prague, everyone knows you're Jewish. Each grave
is a mask. You can stand at the top of the castle, look out over
the orange tiles and cry about your body, what you will return to,
the way she's been hurting you, how you know it has to stop.

Little Voice, Again

Let that never
    happen to me. When you left

those burnt corners of the north, you thought
    you could forget, mostly-white girl.

And then, sudden as a torn poster stuck
    to a lamppost for a vigil,

you saw this was bigger than the motel,
    the car ride, and that awful phone call

from the mother of the girl whose name
    you can't say anymore.

You unfold this story, the last quiet shadow
    of your life she hasn't stared into

with that sharp light, and she says,
    That didn't happen. It wasn't

what we all know it was, what you know
    in the part of you that is still thirteen.

This, the last. What rouses you from that long hallway,
    the dark car, the empty room of your childhood

where you are still telling yourself *get out before*
    something bad happens.

AMYGDALA

Whatever happens with us,
your body will haunt mine—
—Adrienne Rich, "(The Floating Poem, Unnumbered)"

CONFESSIONAL

And then she just comes home, admits it. Kitchen glass
    gleam, cat in the grass, summer hanging

its dense white clouds out on the power
    lines. Shattered blue mosaic

of countertop, her shirtsleeves rolled up
    red and checkered. Midafternoon

and five o'clock nowhere. You have prised this
    apart, together, at last:

If she hurt you enough for you to leave,
    she wouldn't have to be one. *One of them.*

You. But you stayed, and she's still one of you.
    Down goes the wall, without trumpets.

The sun, quiet on the windows. It has nothing
    to do with her father. The boyfriends.

The man nearly her husband. *It has nothing to do
    with you,* she says. Nothing.

The world taught her to hate it—
    herself—and you became the vessel.

Nothing to do with it. As if this shame she poured
    into you won't spill out into other hands, years

later. As if you were just there, could have been
    any other girl. As if you just happened to be

deep enough to catch all the doctors, the names
    they call her, the men who stare and mutter—

as if it had nothing to do with her. It's so easy not to blame
    her. You'll get there. Trust me.

HOUSE OF MIRRORS

You can say it, we already know
    they start to tell you,

roommate and friend, just when
    you start to think it was all

in your head—her hand sliding quick between
    your legs when you stood up to leave her

for the very last time, how she found you
    at your mother's house, told you to lie down,

and you thought, this is how women die—
    just when you start to think

the truth of your body isn't enough,
    the softness, their faces a curtain

lifting, they've been watching
    all along, telling you in their own way

or turning away, one by one, until the truth
    of your story is enough.

AMYGDALA

It names you gazelle and it calls
lion. Stomach churn and lung-hover,
it reroutes the canal of your breath
to quadriceps, large muscle clusters,
the limbs you hold closer

when the flowers arrive it says *fire
alarm*. When the new lover or victim
sits in the front row it says *brimstone*
and it says *yes* to tequila and *yes*
to shaking, always, knees and hands,
under the arm of another woman it will name
safety, it says *go home with her*, you must

go home, avoid the tall grass and public
places, the darkened lot, the stampede
of small crowds and also solitude, go home,

the amygdala says this
is the savannah and you,
a gazelle.

CRESCENTS

Every thirty days you lay down on the floor
swollen and clotted, each begging for relief,
chamomile, advil.

You learned each other so well—
she knew the spot at the small of your back
where the moon takes your tailbone in her fist
and squeezes.

You knew exactly how to fold her leg
across her chest to get into the place
where the ache lives.

Even when you knew it was over
and you left the house, the snow
settled around red leaves, still

your bodies were almost the same,
trying always to create
a new story.

GHOST HOUSE, AGAIN (THE HANGED MAN)

You knew better and disappeared into it
    anyway. The house was waiting

up for you all those nights, with its women
    who laughed, loud wallpaper, the men

who threw you over their shoulders
    like a sack of flour, a small animal, or

a friend. The house never
    looked twice. Nothing made it

blink, the only thing you've ever
    broken into. Didn't you deserve

its wall against your fist, your body ferris-
    wheeled across the floor?

Do you remember that night when everyone
    went separately out onto the balcony, swore

they saw the hanged man? You talked about
    that ghost for years. Practically asked for it.

But it's not your fault. Only the house
    could have seen that first hand
about to cut you down.

FLOATING POEM
after Adrienne Rich

There are two nightmares. The first,
obvious—she is doing it again,

and the second. The second is worse.
You are at work, or walking, near

clear as waking, and she finds you.
She does not speak. In this dream, she holds

her hands out, towards you. She is
crying. She doesn't say

anything, in this dream. She has heard
everything. She knows, and she denies

nothing. She holds her hands out, in
this dream, and you do not take them.

There are two nightmares. This one
is the worst.

APPRENTICE

Anything that makes you feel
    powerful helps, and sometimes

that is push-ups and sometimes a swim
    to cool off and twelve hours

of dreamless sleep, and sometimes it's night
    driving, but sometimes it is also

wine and climbing barefoot onto the balcony
    of a party where you are already high

and need to be coaxed down from the ledge.
    Sometimes it is the kind of power

where no one can stop you from anything,
    which isn't power here

at all.

HOROSCOPE

This week, you try glamour—

buy flowers for the empty
apartment, call your *girlfriends.*

(Not her. The kind for giggling
and lipstick.)

They chop off your hair
in the kitchen, sweep up
the dead ends,

bring housewarming gifts:
the short-stemmed martini glasses
and small orange platyfish

all of which you later break, or kill
in the dish soap accident.

Every time someone mentions her name
you make them say you're pretty.

They make you say *useful.*
They make you say *smart.*

Sugar on the rim of the glass.

No Lack of Love

But sometimes there *is*, you want
    to tell them. Sometimes,

there just isn't enough of you to go
    around, you say, but they weigh

your breasts in their hands and don't
    believe you. You're from a bitter,

bitter place. Everyone was hungry,
    could see a new face coming from a mile away.

Towns licked their teeth and gleamed
    for you, ready. You'll never recover

from that kind of devotion. Little lights in rows
    waiting, patient, to devour you
one by one.

THE DREAM IN WHICH HER FATHER
APPEARS IN MINIATURE

Of course you were afraid of him. All that time, cowered,
    throwing salt to the cows to prove

you loved his daughter in this place, all gravel
    and no water. Not even your own father did you ever

call *sir*, but you swore by it with him, through
    the names he spat, through *faggot*, through *pot-licker*,

Christ-killer, Jewess. Palm-sized man. You thought you could earn
    his approval. When at last it settled

around you, the horses would eat from your hands,
    barn owls light on her shoulders.

Oh, he knew you were a *nice girl*. How hard
    it would be when she left you, for a man, he said.

You tried to fix it, his broken fence, to lift
    the cord of wood into his pickup, polished

grey as a barrel, and he called you *pretty
    weak*. He wasn't wrong. You weren't made to carry his family,

their awful burden, their stolen land, the drink and
    the unspeakable. Children have drowned here in the same

pasture where the wild snapdragons grow, the bees crawling, matted
    and heavy with gold. He's gone crooked, old, and still he crunches

past them all in his black boots, his barbed wire and spurs, iron brand
for what's his and a bullet for the ferals. In time, one of you

would have killed the other. You see him now, at the foot of the coulee,
crotch-bound, shutting in the creatures for the night,

measuring time by what he does not do, anymore. You see him,
shrinking into the arms of his own hills, hidden, while you pull

away slowly from this place where you never
belonged, or wanted to.

THE DESCENT

I wanted what had happened
to be a wall to burn, a window to smash.
At my fist the pieces would sparkle and fall.
All would be changed. I would not be alone.
—*Minnie Bruce Pratt, "Justice, Come Down"*

TEMPERANCE

The night you first pulled me down into
    your bed I wouldn't kiss you, and though

it stopped there, for years later when you were angry
    you'd show me: *This is what it felt like*

when you wouldn't kiss me, this is how awful
    it felt. This is how you taught me

anything I used to protect myself would become
    hurtful, and so I chose

the smallest of shields—a patch of street
    light, the lamp that hangs in

the apartment foyer across the street, a white
    globe that will do in absence

of the moon, nail polish the colour of
    an amaryllis, and the one far carrel

in the library. Except you found me there,
    once, and kissed me so sweetly

I was startled, and you asked for the first time
    ever, and still too late, *Was that ok?*

Nine Swords

I remember lying under your drunk, white
    body while the snow fell, watching the crows land on the power

lines, thinking *This is what everyone*
    wants. This is love. I remember trying to speak plainly.

You tried, too. *Sorry I kinda raped you*
    last night. To finally hear that word from your mouth. You fishtailed

home from pitchers with that awful man,
    another one of your vulturing friends: *How will your girlfriend feel*

about you coming home like this? How will your girlfriend
    feel—He was into it. You were, too. Don't lie. And me,

half-asleep, resistant still. Good job, body—
    this body, your secret, your shadow. *Your sister?* everyone asked.

It's amazing what people will want
    to believe. What I do and don't remember: easing myself down

your stairs in the morning, that your hands were painful, that it was
    my fault. It was always my fault. And I laughed at you,

that word, at first, unbelieving
    even myself.

Banishing

after Daphne Gottlieb's "you never forget your first"

Now that I know what to call
what you did, this time I'll tell you

to stop. Now that I know what to call what
you did, come back and I'll do it right this time,

police and the whole no, the hospital
and changed locks, the story I'll have to tell

three times until anyone believes me and
I give us all a bad name. Now that I know

what to call what you did, get back here
because nothing I ever do will be enough

to prove it.

FILL IN THE BLANKS

Don't freak out, _____.
> *it's just me*
> *it's not like she hit you*

Every time we do something, _____.
> *I feel like I can't touch you*
> *I'm afraid it's your first*

That just makes me _____.
> *see red*
> *want to smack you around even more*
> *think about guns*

I can't believe you _____.
> *would let that happen*
> *could let that happen*
> *let that happen*

Virgin, or The Woman You Think Is Me

If you can't have it, at least I should give you
    the story of how it was taken.

But that relic is long gone, and when I give you
    no instead, you hoof & paw, blow

inlets of steam until I know you. You're that noble
    creature, single-minded, sharp-browed,

who can only be captured by a woman *untouched.*
    The woman you think is me.

We can pretend if you really want to. Each of us
    is a myth. You lay your head

in my lap like you're a unicorn, & I'm something
    I haven't been in a very long time.

VISITATIONS

That winter I promised I would
be no one's secret, and yet

there you were like a lock, shining,
a hook on every story I wouldn't have

to tell. In your attic room you sang
to me and were a different kind

of rural, you knew what it was to
be mispronounced. We even knew

each other, once, when we were small
and in your even smaller town—I remember,

I checked the yellow figure-skating program
again and again for your name. And here,

in the so-called city, you hadn't even met
the girl who did what she did to me.

Blessed ignorance. When she appeared
at the bar, I thought of your hand

tucked against my waist where
no one would never see. And when

she appeared at the bookstore,
I thought of your attic room, and your

ways of hiding, how your parents
would never need to know me.

And when she appeared at the neighbour
girl's, or in the parking lot

we never used that word, *stalked,*
though I cut my hair, changed

licence plates, phone number. Some people
wait all their lives to see a woman just *appear*

like that. And when I was
afraid of her, or any surprise, I thought

of you coming in from the cold, unexpected,
your glasses fogged and the gold buttons

at the neck of your coat and your heels
against the ice. Or at my door after a late flight,

asking me if I was scared. You weren't scared.
And when she appeared at the door to my mother's

house, I breathed, and counted, and thought of you,
and your invisible parents, there on the rocks

at Medjugorje, your bright faith
in some good apparition.

WHEN IT WAS GOOD

I wanted it to be like this, with her,
    always—the night at the ranch, where

after she had touched me like I was
    precious, there was that soft

tin sound of the screen door, the sky
    spilled across itself into dark and

unabashed with stars. Raccoons out
    with their small whinnies, sparrow

trills, me with my arms around her waist, she
    named the sounds I didn't know yet,

telling me there was nothing
    to be afraid of.

I've never seen anything so bright
    and possible. Promised

I would pretend that time was our first.
    Sometimes, I still do,

even in this place where you are
    holding my hand so tightly

while she walks in and out of my body
    and I tell you about the raccoons, instead.

DEATH BROUGHT YOU BACK

If death hadn't brought you back
into my life, I might even have forgiven

you. Not anymore. And when the phone call
came, you knew it. *I am so sorry,* you told me.

*I am so sorry that it's me who has
to tell you.* I wasn't sorry. If this

was the world's way of sealing you off
from me, wrapped in the memory

of death, so be it. How awful, the way
you are in this memory—telling me

about death, about love, and days
later pushing me down the stairs

in my mother's own house, telling me
to lie down while I curl into this chair

she still owns, while I tell you no
again and again until you stop just

short. You ruined this, our precious
week of mourning, and I remember also

how you came back, how you cried
and told me you regretted everything.

Do you remember how my mother
made you coffee, and fed you and your

collection of orphaned friends, and that
she knew, eventually, she and my father,

and they wished me a host of new people
to love me instead of these lost boys, back

when I was still trying to learn to be gay
from boys, and my mother and father

did not kill you, they fed you, and then
I hated you—with my mother's blue mug in your hands,

on my step with your tears and inadequate
regret, you and how you got yourself into this memory.

When I say your name my friends can still
see your face. Hello, fresh hell.

This is how I know I believe
my own story—that even when I think

a part of me should still love you, even
a little, I want the world to burn before

you come close to anyone I love again,
even with your kind self.

And over that bonfire I wondered,
how am I here with you, and at that wake

I prayed for you to be anyone else, and also
I knew that this would be among my last memories

of you, at last. The beginning of some
new power, and I refused to speak to you

the whole way home. And I remember
you crossed the lawn to me at the memorial,

and I remember Liz and Amy leading me out
into the field across the wire fence and into the tall

grass to cry. And I remember thinking, later,
I will tell them what you've done. And then

I remember nothing, except driving everyone
we loved, minus you, back into the city,

and how the sky was flat and blue, and the sun
was in the ditch, and that

death had brought you back, and I was finally
getting away.

MONOTHEISM

It takes three years
    to forget her. The first, I circle

seven times to cast out the devil. Crush it, glass
    beneath my heel. Lift the veil. Say,

this was not the bride I wanted. Until I sound
    like I mean it, canopied and alone.

The second, I leave behind. Burning,
    disastrous, a trail of salt

from my own pillar. What I turned when
    I turned back.

The third, I arrive at the doorstep
    of her memory, smear it

in blood. Somewhere,
    I call another woman

by her name, on purpose.

AMULET

I keep one amulet from our years
    as an evil eye—I need to keep you

far away but your memory real and near,
    for now. There's a whole box to choose from, dust

and old gifts. I take the smallest, a bone worn down
    like a sea stone, notched on its back. Dinosaur

vertebrae—like you, something so old, and so big, once
    I can hardly believe it existed.

THE FIRST WOMAN WHO DOESN'T

Is a museum where I think, *not again*—
    the morning, the bottle of whiskey
in my purse, no memory of empty.

Helps me bend down into my headache
    and dig for the same old shards—
where I shed the ghost of my clothes,

how, the bruise steepled across my leg,
    why, the door left wide open,
the inexplicable staircase.

Doesn't laugh at my bad joke
    about *taking advantage*.

Tells me about the skyline
    I never will remember.

Waited for my heaving to turn
    to sleep, can't believe

I thought she'd touch me when
    I was unconscious, can't believe

I've spent my life with women
    who would. Waits for me

to tell her about it, and listens.

BRUISES

This was not an original practice,

but thinking for a time, that it was
felt like being able to choose

when spring would arrive
—Sara Peters, "The Last Time I Slept in This Bed"

The new rule was that if it hurt
        and I wanted it,

I had to ask someone to do it for me.
        And so I never asked. The first time

it's an accident—I am perpetually
        drunk, full of adrenaline and

You like pain, she marvels
        at me, astounded by my threshold

for spring. A whole week I can't sleep
        on my front, wear a push-up bra,

hug tight. Frozen peas, frozen
        corn, one defrosted bottle

of gin, a thirty-second panic in the shower
        thinking *I wanted this,* one acceptable

rock in my pocket. The new
        rule. The next time, it's a surprise

for us both, *for such gentle
        creatures,* pointed out

under sleeves or backless, in warm weather,
        like I've been in out

in the sun. Look how much
        you love me. Little maps. *Look,*

you tell me,
        we match, all spring.

INVOCATION
for _____

It takes me a week of sweat to call you
what your parents did. A football coach,
I barked your surname instead, feigned fraternity.

The housemates shudder when I tell them
about you. *Not that one,* I swear, but still
it echoes.

It's not your fault. Your first
was popular in the eighties.
And it's not spelled the same
way. Right?

Right. I sit and breathe
in the outs of your cigarettes. Listen
to our names called together
without a shiver.

When you say *Leah,* I make myself
call you back. Your name. Not *hers.*

I dig the sound of her name out
from the burnt house of my mouth
like a gold tooth.

I hold it up to the light.
It rings when I swallow.
The sound of your name—

yours,
and mine.

CROWS

In the dream of the new house, I have my own window
    facing west: cherry blossom and fig trees,

monkey puzzle and magnolia. Everything flowers.
    Whatever city this is will be good to me.

And then, the crows, tiny shreds of black cloth
    thrown over the sunset, and I think the world

is ending. A kind hand tells me, this is the largest murder
    in North America. If I ride my bike far enough,

I can roost with them at night, east beneath the mountain.
    A stray crow wings away from the path of feathers, back

towards the squares of land I imagine, flat and brooding.
    You're going the wrong way, crow! Come back!

But she was never really going, and I watch as she returns
    with that other bird, as dark and near as her own shadow.

LIBERATION
for mt

I'm tired of it, you tell me,
    having known this truth of your body

since skinned knees and recess. Now, I watch
    the green in your eyes fleck as you discover

those other stories hidden in your own old country,
    what your mother knows she has to tell you.

There's only so much time, you say. How those archives
    of cell and helix will falter with age

and secrecy, new language and distance. I know.
    I'm tired of my body too, in a different way,

the stories I feel I have to keep telling
    for *the revolution.* It's like I haven't stopped

grieving or fighting long enough to notice
    your hands—and then you put one over your chest,

and the other over mine, small and empty, and say
    you know where liberation really is.

And I want that, with you, the truth
    of our bodies, even when we're tired,

before we forget.

LEVITATING

You and me in the tree fort, like I was
    the eighteen I always wanted.

And the harbour quiet below us,
    little crowns of light and rain

on water. The train that rattled past,
    you kissing me, the woods,

and the dark, my first real *yes*
    in a long, long time.

MAGIC

All of a sudden I know it's not
going to happen. And panic, silent
until I remember—you're not her, I could just

ask you to stop. Except that you already
have, and wait, and listen while my body
tells me a very old story.

You don't ask questions, unless
I want them, and I want anything
but these red eyes that look out

from mine like the forest, anything but
this silence. When you tell me that this
look like strength to you, how you love this

about me, I almost hate you. Why do you
have to be so good? This has to be magic, how
you hold me while I turn into a snake and fire

and grief itself beneath you. *Good magic,*
you tell me, and don't ask any questions
until I want them.

A Woman Taught You to Do This

To be *careful*. And a woman tried
to teach me I didn't deserve it,

that no one
would believe me.

And a woman who maybe no one believed
taught you to see it—

those dark circles, how I want quiet,
the sweetness of your hands, an end to panic.

When I go to tell you the truth, you're waiting there
for me with your arms out, like you've known

all along. Maybe you did. Not in the way I'm afraid of,
written on me in a language reserved

for disasters. Of course you just know.
A woman taught you to do this,

and nothing I can say will surprise you, except
that I already love you

here on the flat of your chest while the last train
of my old story

rattles past and howls for me. I can barely hear it
over the sound of you, breathing.

A woman taught you to do this, while
a woman tried to teach me

I didn't deserve it, and the truth is we've been
waiting here to tell each other, all along.

CROWS, AGAIN

Well, this is it. Vancouver, the city
    I dreamed. Winter will never

be the same here—the roses just curling to wilt
    when it's nearly spring, the shaving

of frost from windshields between hydrangea.
    We can have the ocean and the patch

of white at the crest of the mountain, those lights
    all crooked together like tips of quartz.

Every time, on that walk under the shreds of feathers
    at sundown, someone's arm

slung around me or just the light, another exhale,
    a little more, what I didn't know I still held.

ANNIVERSARY

It has taken five years and fifteen hundred
    kilometres to get away, and closer

to the mountains. I can see them—
    every day, like I always wanted. Near,

and distant. Every day I can ask people
    not to touch me—

on the bus, on the beach, or in my new kitchen.
    Or, I could ask them to—

which, lately, is harder. How can it still
    feel so soon? She has never been

near this new body of mine—
    short-haired, tattooed, very strong

and very, very fast, now. I carry a chunk of rose
    quartz the size of my thumb for safety.

I have sworn to myself a life of people
    who know when to stop. I promised—

and spent my first night in the new apartment drawing
    circles in salt and rain, whispering

to my old self, *come here. I built this*
    for you. I promised.

CONCLUSION

This book is a journey that began many years ago, now.

I was nineteen when my first girlfriend sexually assaulted me. I had been out as a lesbian for a year or two; I had allied parents and queer friends and was more than halfway through a minor in gender studies. I was aware of women in the news who had been violent—who abused children, or who killed their abusive, male partners. But the idea that a relationship between two women could be abusive—that *my* relationship might have been abusive—eluded me. How could this *happen*?

Like many survivors, I was desperate for any representation of my own story—but I found nothing. I was a freak. I made women do things women aren't supposed to do—be sexually violent. *It was my fault, I deserved it.* When I finally sought help after months of paranoia, anxiety, and PTSD, the counsellor told me, "You sound exactly like a woman who was raped by a man."

I was destroyed. Wasn't it different, when it was a woman? I wanted it to be different. I was terrified. If I told people that queers hurt each other, they'd think we were *just like everyone else.* If I called out another woman for a behaviour most likely rooted in her own trauma, then I was being a *bad feminist.* If I told people that a white queer woman called me racist names, and laughed about how her ancestors probably colonized mine, people would say, *It's not like she hit you.*

I felt like I couldn't talk to anyone—so I read. Where were my lesbian feminist foremothers when I needed them? I turned to zines: *Support,* by Cindy Crabb, *Learning Good Consent* from Philly's Pissed, and *The Revolution Starts At Home.* I read Chrystos, who was writing about queer violence in the S/M community years ago. I went to the Lesbian Herstory Archives in Brooklyn and found entire subject folders about violence between queer women.

But I still couldn't find anything about rape perpetrated by lesbians. In the absence of those materials, I found what I was looking for—affirmation that stories of queer in-community sexual assault need to be told. We need these stories: so we can love one another without re-perpetuating our trauma, and so we can build communities where we can heal. We need these stories so we can live.

Many things have happened since I first came out about my experience. I have been accused of being an alarmist—that my experience wasn't *real rape*. A number of people online have devoted considerable time to the curious legal implications of my experience. I have also been sexually assaulted again, by women: once, classically, while blacked out at a house party, and many times when I have been nonconsensually touched by women who believe that they have access to me because of my femme gender and my "exotic" body. I have also connected with many brilliant, articulate racialized and dis/Abled youth, trans* women, and sex workers who have always been at the forefront of calling out queer in-community violence—because they overwhelmingly experience the most severe, isolating, sexualized, and fatal abuse at the hands of our own so-called queer and feminist "communities."

More than anything, on this particular journey, I have been met with the generous and brave disclosure of many other queer survivors and allies. This is a privilege, I know, due to many intersections of my identity. It is a privilege to have my experience acknowledged, even as it has been a struggle. I am grateful to the legacy of queer in-community survivors who have come before me—and who will come, for there is much work to do yet. I am grateful to queer survivors, our allies, and elders for keeping me here, in and beyond my survival. This book is for them.

ACKNOWLEDGEMENTS

These poems were lived, written, and performed on Treaty Six Cree territory and the unceded lands of the Musqueam, Tsleil-Waututh, and Skwxwú7mesh people.

Early versions of these poems appeared in *Adrienne, the Bakery, Cactus Heart, CutBank, Canadian Poetries, Plenitude,* and *Force Field: 77 Women Poets of British Columbia.* My gratitude to the editors of each.

The epigraphs at the beginning of each section and selected poems are from, in order of appearance: Sharon Olds's "I Go Back to May 1937"; Louise Glück's "October"; Adrienne Rich's "(The Floating Poem, Unnumbered)" in "Twenty-One Love Poems"; "Justice, Come Down" by Minnie Bruce Pratt; Sara Peters, "The Last Time I Slept in This Bed." My humble gratitude and respect to the authors of each. The Michelle Tea poem referenced in "Suit of Feathers" is "Gazpacho," from *The Beautiful: Collected Poems.* The line "Now that I know what to call/what you did" in "Banishing" is from Daphne Gottlieb's "you never forget your first" from *Why Things Burn.* The line "I remember trying to speak plainly" is after Dorothy Allison's *Two or Three Things I Know For Sure.* "Hello, fresh hell" is a variation on an oft-quoted phrase by Dorothy Parker. My gratitude to the artists and writers behind the *Collective Tarot,* whose visionary work is also referenced with honour throughout the collection.

Special mention must be made of Rhea Tregebov, who believed in this difficult project from the beginning; Keith Maillard, for his resounding final approval; my colleagues in the UBC creative writing MFA program; and the staff at UBC Graduate Research Awards for partial funding of my research trip to New York City.

Invaluable support for this project was provided by Dolores Cennon at the Saskatoon Sexual Assault and Information Centre;

Joanne Horsley at the Avenue Community Centre in Saskatoon; Jennifer Patterson of *Queering Sexual Violence*; July Westhale and T.T. Jax of the forthcoming anthology *Fresh Meat: Trans/Queer Survivors on In-Community Assault.* Lori B. Girshick's *Woman-to-Woman Sexual Violence: Does She Call It Rape* and *The Revolution Starts At Home* (edited by Leah Lakshmi Piepzna-Samarasinha, Ching-In Chen, and Jai Dulani) were vital texts during my healing process. Gratitude to Laneia, Stephanie, and the team at *Autostraddle.com* for publishing my first online account of this experience and to Saskia, Rachel, and the volunteers at the the Lesbian Herstory Archives for their assistance with research.

Love to Tony and Jen at the the Lambda Literary Foundation, and the Poetry Fellows of the 2012 LGBT Literary Retreat. To Jewelle Gomez and Dorothy Allison, in awe and gratitude. To Maxim Backer and Abbie J. Leavens for the gift of their friendship. Thanks to Billeh Nickerson, Sean Cranbury, Alex Leslie, Daniel Zomparelli, Chris Gilpin, and Jillian Christmas for all their work creating literary spaces where this work could take hold in Vancouver.

Amber Dawn, Rachel Rose, Andrea Routley, and the dream team at Caitlin Press have made the process of this book gentle, and I cannot thank them enough.

My life and these poems are richer for the love and support of Adrienne Gruber, Hilary Smith, Melanie Matining, Anoushka Ratnarajah, Jen Sung, Nadine Boulay, Mik Turje, Amy Dyck, Calondra Mainhart, Sarah York, Amy Huziak, Alison Roth Cooley, Robyn Kretschmann, Megan Van Buskirk, and Rachel Fowlie-Neufeld. To Esther McPhee, who I will love forever, for holding my hand through this entire project. To my parents, my brother, my grandparents, and ancestors, who have stayed with me every moment of this journey. *A sheynem dank.*

Leah Horlick is a writer and poet from Saskatoon. A 2012 Lambda Literary Fellow in Poetry, she holds an MFA in creative writing from the University of British Columbia. Her first collection of poetry, *Riot Lung* (Thistledown Press, 2012), was shortlisted for a 2013 ReLit Award and a Saskatchewan Book Award. She lives on Unceded Coast Salish Territories in Vancouver, where she co-curates REVERB, a queer and anti-oppressive reading series.

This book is set in Arno Pro, designed by Robert Slimbach.
The text was typeset by Benjamin Dunfield.
Caitlin Press, Spring 2015.

🌿